ITALIAN MAJOLICA

I. FAENZA. BEGINNING OF THE FIFTEENTH CENTURY

ITALIAN MAJOLICA

TEXT BY JIŘINA VYDROVÁ

*

PHOTOGRAPHS BY JOSEF EHM

*

TRANSLATED BY OTA VOJTÍŠEK

*

PETER NEVILL

DESIGN BY KAREL VODÁK

46114

DESIGNED AND PRODUCED BY ARTIA FOR

PETER NEVILL

SPRING HOUSE • SPRING PLACE • LONDON N W 5

© 1960 BY ARTIA

S 870

'They please me by their perfection and rarity, being quite novelties in these parts and are valued more than if of silver, the donor's arms serving daily to recall their origin.'

IN THESE WORDS Lorenzo Magnifico thanked Robert Malatesta in 1490 for his gift of ceramics, namely Italian majolica, artistic products of Italian potters which at that time—in the same way as the delicate Murano glass, and even before that the luxurious Italian silk fabrics—gained the favour of Renaissance society and began to make famous the skill of Italian artist-craftsmen far beyond the frontier of their country.

The history of majolica, however, begins long before that time.

While in the countries north of the Alps pottery remained for a long time on the level of a primitive handicraft, the Italians as early as the fourteenth century tried to produce ceramic ware of artistic value. Their commercial relations with countries with an old ceramic tradition, that is Asia and the Arabian territories in the Mediterranean, enabled them earlier than any other European country to acquaint themselves with and to master the well-developed production methods of the Orient. From the East, from Persia, came first the practice of covering the surface of the biscuit with a white layer of clay (engobe), the decor being executed on it either by means of engraved lines or with coloured earth, and protection being given by a thin layer of opaque, lustrous lead glazing. The excellent properties of the soft white Vicenza and Sienna clay facilitated this process, and it developed at the turn of the fifteenth and sixteenth centuries in the region between the Adriatic Sea in the east and inland between Padua, Bologna and Perugia. Characteristic were vessels with engraved (*sgraffiato*) decor of stylised Gothic leaves and Renaissance figures.

In competition with this simple pottery technique of 'semi-majolica' or 'imitation faience'— for that is the technical designation of engobe ceramics—another method of production, which appeared somewhat later, prevailed. More advanced in development, technically more refined and artistically more pleasing, it was the true majolica. The rough biscuit was no

7

longer covered with the delicate engobe which peeled off easily, but with a stannic, completely non-porous and opaque white glaze which, in the high heat of the kiln, blended with the painting directly executed in it into a hard, lustrous layer, adhering to the clay foundation.

Masters of this technique, which required great experience and skill, were the Arabian Moors. They found in Spain, where they were living at that time, rich deposits of tin which provided an exceptionally favourable local raw material for the development of their ceramic production. The spontaneous artistic feeling of the Arabian craftsman manifested itself in the beauty of the decor, usually painted blue, and embellished on the surface with lustrous, iridescent, metallic colours. The golden shine of their ceramics was perhaps to them a poor substitute for the vessels of precious metal which Mohammed's teaching forbade them to use, but they traded successfully with this ware of such striking beauty to other eyes. From the Balearic Islands ships sailed for the Italian ports of Genoa and Pisa, laden with their fragile, sparkling goods, which in Italy were popularly called Majolica, named from the port of Majorca, from where they were exported. The name of majolica soon became a technical term for all similar Italian wares. Already in 1454 mention is made in Faenza of a producer of 'white majolica'.

It is not known when exactly the Italians themselves started to produce majolica ware. As early as 1330 Pietro del Bono of Pola in his work, *Margarita preciosa*, lists tin as the main component of potter's glaze, but the first dated relic—a jug with the arms of Astorigo Manfredi, Lord of Faenza, from the end of the fourteenth century—would suggest by its primitive technique of execution that production was then just beginning.

It was only in the fifteenth century that the universal spreading of Renaissance plastic art brought about also artistic development of majolica. In spite of the fact that the production of, and interest in, majolica was steadily growing, its importance was not yet very great. For over fifty years majolica ware remained for the most part utilitarian pottery of good quality. The impermeable walls of the vessels, the outward and inside smooth enamel, which could be easily washed, caused the white enamelled vessels to be used above all for pharmaceutical purposes. And, as in the Orient, these long-necked bulbous pots, these convex vessels with small handles and the cylindrical, slender albarella (whose name, derived from the Persian

8

el barani or 'spice container', reveals its original function) served for the storing of spices, balsams, ointments and oils.

Both the shapes and decor show the influence of the East. Among foreign ornaments of stylised leaves, usually cut in stripes, there also appear frequently inscriptions with names of drugs written in Gothic letters or Roman type. Sometimes the mark of crutches or a ladder with a cross show that the vessels belonged to the hospital pharmacy of the Santa Maria Nuova cloister or the Santa Maria della Scala cloister in Florence, the largest, richest and oldest monastic hospitals in Italy.

From among the many preserved relics from the first two thirds of the fifteenth century, only one single group is conspicuously different and we can judge, at least approximately, from which region it originated. It contains urn-shaped, massive vessels, frequently with small handles, finished with a milky or dirty white enamel decorated with pastose painting in dark blue cobalt, which is not found anywhere else. A slender twig with oak leaves is freely wound round the concave walls of the vessels, frequently decorated in front with large Gothic lettering, the mark of a monastery or a figuration or animal motif. The place of origin of this majolica ware, so impressive by reason of the directness of the painter's expression, is considered to be Castel Fiorentino near Florence, where many such fragments have been found. It seems also, that the lily blossom which adorns the vessel in the Victoria and Albert Museum in London and a similar one in the North Bohemian Museum at Liberec, is not a chance design, but that it is connected with the heraldic lily of the Florentine Republic.

About the middle of the fifteenth century, when the Florentine workshops produced these unusually impressive vessels, the Florentine sculptor Luca della Robbia made his first experiments by applying tin enamels on large terra-cotta reliefs for the adornment of Florentine buildings and intended, according to Vasari, also for the interior of the Medici Palace. History has disproved the legend which considered Luca as the inventor of majolica. But he must be acknowledged as the first who dared, in a truly adventurous manner, to use the experience of his predecessors on large plastic works and, in addition, he was apparently the first in Italy to use multi-coloured enamel.

As a sculptor Luca had a limited range of subjects; the filling of lunettes and round medallions framed with wreaths of fruit and flowers with the figure of the Madonna or the saints, always executed in high relief with the application of all colours which could be fired at high temperatures, were his speciality. Luca's successors in the following century were Andrea and Giovanni, who carried on the ceramic tradition of the workshop far into the sixteenth century. From Andrea's workshop indubitably originated the large wreath-framed medallion with the coat of arms of Baptista Bartolomeus Debenuci from the year 1517, which is the property of the Museum of Industrial Art in Prague.

However, the sculptural ceramic style of Robbia found only a slight response beyond the circle of his workshop, mainly in the somewhat naive compositions of other now anonymous workshops from the end of the fifteenth and the beginning of the sixteenth century. Their themes are mostly biblical, composed from now unknown period paintings. The ambitious efforts of these craftsmen are testified to by the large relief 'The Adoration of the Kings' in the Prague Museum of Industrial Art, where an unknown artist dealt successfully as regards technique and execution with the complications of composition with an intricate background of human and animal figures.

The production of majolica ware continued independently of the achievements of Luca's workshop. The developments which progressed very slowly in the first half of the fifteenth century showed increased activity in the second half. Man learned to employ things not only to serve him, but to embellish his life, and he surrounded himself in his home with beautiful *objets d'art*. In this atmosphere where the striving after elegance became the essence of life, where taste was refined and old values re-appraised, pottery became a fine art. The simple handicraft which until then had supplied only domestic wares for everyday use, rose to become a universally admired artistic activity. The simple, serviceable majolica products changed as it were into the coveted artistic pieces. In the house they were prominently displayed. They were used for the decoration of the table and sideboard on festive occasions and to own these *piatti di pompa* and to present them to friends was the fashion. They were often used as flower-vases and flower-pots and as such they can frequently be seen reproduced in Vittore Carpaccio's pictures.

The number of kinds of majolica increased, too. Besides the slim albarello, which for centuries had been used in pharmacies, there were made, for the same purpose, low-necked, round vessels, belly-shaped bottles with long necks and pear-shaped jugs with a tubular spout. For the decoration of the home there were two-handled vases—really especially large plates with an almost hat-shaped cross-section and a small convex bottom and large broad rim. All these types are characterised by the geometrical simplicity of shapes turned on the potter's wheel. But the most significant sign of advanced development is the decor itself. By this time the potter-painters had mastered their craft perfectly. They painted with a steady hand in precise, sharp contours in unusually rich, deep, impressive colours. The style of this majolica ware is justly called 'austere'.

In the frequently occurring figure motives the painters sometimes use folk woodcut models, but the ornament is created by the workshop decorators themselves. At first it is the unconven- 2 tional decor of stiff, broad leaves, terminating in a spiral curve, usually combined with a lithe animal figure in front, as we can see on the bulbous vessel from about 1450-70 with the figure of a strutting bird from the collection of the Museum of Industrial Art at Brno. Later on the II design was superseded by an ornament which is a free interpretation of various traditional elements, 'Gothic' foliage and tendrils, early Renaissance motifs of palmettes, rosettes, scales, coins, leaf wreaths with antique heads, fashionable period motifs of peacock feathers and finally of stone pine-cones and pomegranates. This was a fashionable design for contemporary Italian fabrics, inspired by the Orient.

Modern man's conception of Italian majolica as a characteristic national artistic expression is formed from these products, in which the creative power of the Italian people found expression in this way for the first time. It left a unique imprint also on other Italian contem- 4 porary works of art. In these late Quattrocento majolica wares we perceive primarily strong, vigorous, racially individual features which we do not meet in the same measure in the later French faiences and even less in the Delft ceramics, which owe their fame rather to an elaboration of Chinese designs than to creative invention.

The bizarre beauty of Italian colours and painting, together with the novel technique, paved the way for majolica ware beyond the borders of Italy. They penetrated along with Italian culture into Hungary to the Buda Court of Matthias Corvinus, which was at that time an outstanding centre of Italian culture. In the Victoria and Albert Museum in London there are two plates from a service, ordered most probably in 1476 by Corvinus at Faenza on the occasion of his marriage to Beatrice of Naples, on which the arms of the royal couple are incorporated into an ornament which is a complex of all characteristic motifs of that time. In the eighties of the fifteenth century the new style of expression is already stabilized. Its typical elements — the scale pattern and leaf wreaths with antique head — appeared in new 3 variations on two large spherical vessels, which originated somewhat later, probably also at Faenza and which are today in the Prague Museum of Industrial Art.

It was not mere chance that Matthias Corvinus chose the Faenza workshops. At that time this old ceramic centre came to the fore and succeeded in holding its leading position in the production of majolica for more than fifty years. The 'austere' style matured here in its classical form and at the beginning of the sixteenth century influenced the production of the Sienna and Medici workshop at Caffaggiolo, until it gradually disappeared in the thirties. From that period there are in the Prague Museum of Industrial Art two long-necked drug-pots on which a severe design of foliage and tendrils surrounds the large figures of Lucretia 8, 9 and Kimeon and Pera. The assured drawing as well as the conventional conception of the landscape in the background connect these two famous pieces with similar flasks in the Victoria and Albert Museum in London and with vessels bearing the arms of Orsi-Colonna in the British Museum.

In the first half of the sixteenth century majolica ware was firmly established in the life of Italian society. It found its most diverse employment in daily life and more than ever it became valuable as gifts and souvenirs. The known shapes were now added to by the so-called wedding-bowls with the figures of the betrothed on them, and especially by *scudelle da donna di parte*, the *accouchement* sets, usually pyramidically arranged according to size, in which, as was then customary, friends brought choice food to women in childbed. They were produced in large numbers and they are not always artistically successful or carefully executed. They are interesting only on account of the subject of the decor, dealing with contemporary life, as in the case of the bowl from the Prague Museum of Industrial Art, where at the base of the vessel 34 there are figures of women with children, and on the lid a scene showing a mother lying in bed.

12

Workshops competed in realising new ideas. New aesthetic conceptions appeared. Towards the middle of the century the manufacture of majolica ware ceased to be a mere potter's craft and assimilated the production technique of other materials—especially metals. In potters' workshops shaping in plaster forms was introduced. The surface of vessels acquired an expressive relief by means of groups and plastic embossing imitating the effects of wrought metal.   22

An outstanding example of this kind is a dish, from 1530—1540, with the dark blue *turchino*   16 glaze from the Museum of Industrial Art at Brno. Its surface is divided by hollow petals, obliquely and radially arranged around an elevated centre, and a circularly raised, narrow, straight rim is almost a literal imitation of contemporary Venetian decorative dishes, enameled on copper or brass.

In the second quarter of the century the *vasi a bronzo antico*, inspired by Italian Renaissance bronzes, with handles in the shape of serpents' bodies and satyrs' or goats' heads were fashionable.

The appearance of majolica ware became more refined. A better prepared clay was fired into a thinner biscuit and the surface was covered with a white or with a coloured glaze—light   14 blue *smaltino* and dark blue *turchino*—these two shades being characteristic of the Faenza and Venetian workshops. The brilliant lustre of the surface was achieved by means of a thin layer of lead glaze. With the lower basic layer the potter mixed fine white clay, which formed a harder, less absorbing and more suitable basis for a complicated method of painting.

But the main change consisted in the painted decor. In contrast with the 'austere style' of former times, with its intense colouring, the new delicate painting began to be appreciated. Instead of plasticity of surfaces and in place of the old variegated colours, a two-colour tone of white and blue gave way, in the second quarter of the century, to spontaneous brush-work and richly displayed colouring of the Urbino period. The decor of majolica ware was no longer a mere painter's improvisation and it became an intentional, exacting, artistic work of specialist painters, who frequently ceased to be modestly anonymous and boldly signed their products with their name or the mark of their workshop.

The painted decor of ceramic ware was never so variegated and rich. At the beginning of the sixteenth century was introduced the grotesque design which had been taken over by

13

Renaissance artists from antiquity, especially from late Roman architecture. It was applied in potters' workshops through the influence of pictorial records by Agostinus Venezianus, Nicoletto da Modena, and others. The simple, formal shapes of the fifteenth century gave place to the realistic paintings and relief decorations of Amorettes, grotesque figures, antique busts, laurel wreaths, musical instruments and especially antique armour. One well-known group of the grotesque designs was named *a trofei*.

Faenza, Caffaggiolo and Castel Durante—a new centre on the Metaurus River near Urbino—competed in applying the new decor. Besides the disciplined severely symmetrical conception of Caffaggiolo, where the design composed round a vertical axis—*a candalieri*—predominated, the Castel Durante workshops created from trophies and musical instruments an asymmetrical design covering the whole surface. In the Museum of Industrial Art in Prague and Liberec there are several vessels with this decor executed with a surface of yellow-grey grisaille painting on a smudged blue background.

The Faenza ateliers, although not consciously avoiding any new trends, preferred from the beginning the gracious Raphael grotesque compositions with their palmettes, dolphins with leafy tails, vase-motifs, open books and labels with lettering. An early example is a dish from about 1520 in the Museum of Industrial Art at Brno, on which the white decor in reserve, and partially scratched into the basic colour, rises on a blue background as a delicately moulded relief of laurel leaves with antique busts, acanthus foliage and baskets with fruit. The emblem of the clasped hands of the man and woman, similarly executed in the middle, implies that it is a nuptial or wedding plate. But the fame of Faenza majolica ware with grotesque compositions was first established by the Pirota workshop—Casa Pirota—with its *a berettino* or *sopra azzuro* technique, in which the grotesques, designed after Raphael and finished in white paint, are executed in reserve in light blue glaze. The delicacy of these designs reminds one— perhaps intentionally—of the lacy charm of contemporary Italian open-work embroideries, *punto tagliato* and *punto tirato*, and ensured the success of the Pirota workshop for more than two decades. The *a berettino* design is almost always combined, at least partially, with a coloured motif; it is either the figure of a lute-player, as on a plate from the Prague Museum of Industrial Art, or Alexander's head as on a plate from the Brno Museum of Industrial Art

14

or a coat of arms on a specimen from the North Bohemian Museum at Liberec. The most remarkable piece of this group in the Czech collections is a large basin from about 1530 in the Brno Museum of Industrial Art, which bears the arms of the Florentine family of Salviati with a painting of fruit in the middle.

The grotesque style is partially connected with another group of majolica ware represented by a bowl from the Liberec Museum. Oblique embossing on its rim is alternately painted blue and orange, with acanthus foliage in reserve. In the white glazed middle there is the figure of an apostle in colours. Cipriano Piccolpasso, the author of a well-known work on the production of majolica ware, who was less well-known as a Castel Durante potter, attributes these vessels to Castel Durante workshops. But as a matter of fact they had also been produced in other workshops, in Faenza to name only one.

A speciality of the Castel Durante workshops in the years 1530—40, which was not repeated anywhere else, was on the one hand opaque white, painted over a greyish-white enamel—*bianco sopra bianco*—and, on the other hand, oak foliage, presumably alluding to the arms of the Rovere family, the lords of Urbino. These two ornaments frequently appear simultaneously on various wares. An example is the large dish from the Brno Museum of Industrial Art, where opaque white decor, framed in an oak sprig with acorns and with the figure of Archangel Michael fighting the devil in the middle, is painted in bright colours. Or again the plate from the Červený Kameň Castle, with the figure of a naked boy with a dog, is a further example.

Another outstanding group is majolica ware with a prevailing plant decor. This group consists above all of utilitarian articles, such as albarellos pharmacy vases, which were produced in the years 1500—1520 at Faenza and are represented by several examples in the Museum of Industrial Art of Prague and Brno and in the Silesian Museum at Opava. In the delicate trail pattern, painted in blue, the 'austere' style is seen gradually to disappear. In the stressed white-blue contrast of decor and background another aesthetic conception becomes apparent. It is remotely inspired by the decorative principle of a new, rare ceramic product—Chinese porcelain, with which European peoples became acquainted through the medium of Persian faiences, influenced in their turn by the Chinese ware. The term *a la porcellana* which appears in the potter's terminology of the period, relates not only to the above-mentioned Faenza albarellos, but also to some Venetian types. In the case of Venetian majolica ware from the beginning of the century, however, the influence of the Orient is more pronounced through the white-and-blue Persian ware with its realistic flora, as well as the *rabeschi* pattern, of elegant, severely stylised tendrils, most probably inspired by damaskeen metal work. On dishes and plates covered with a thick layer of greyish-blue enamel with added cobalt, there appear the elements of these ornaments from Asia Minor in the form of a delicate floral arabesque bordering figural or portrait motifs or coats of arms.

A folie, a frutti, a fiori—foliage, fruit, blossoms—remained during the whole of the sixteenth century typical characteristics of Venetian majolica decoration, but they were becoming ever larger and more Europeanised. In the Museum of Industrial Art in Prague this type, from the second quarter of the century, is represented by a blue plate with wide-spread maple foliage, painted in dark blue, which is a literal replica of two other specimens from the Kunstgewerbemuseum in Berlin. Another one, smaller, with a coat of arms in the middle, is in the Červený Kameň Castle, where there is also a large drug-pot, on the *smaltino* glazing of which is painted the inscription A. D. CICORA and on the back among the foliage a blue drawing of the figure of Mercury.

Venetian plant decor crystallized in the second half of the century in overflowing baroque forms of acanthus leaves, blossoms and fruit. Monochrome design was replaced by painting in rich colours, among them opaque white glazing breaking through a blue ground. Large vessels, large and small albarellos were decorated in reserve by spontaneous brush-work with the heads of Venetian women, old men with turbans, young men with berets and also with the figures of saints. Repeated styles and mannerisms of workmanship betray a considerable workshop production, based on a limited supply of models. The best pieces are connected with the name of Domenigo Veneziano, working in Venice between 1560–70. A large albarello with the picture of 'Beautiful Cornelia', owned by the Museum of Industrial Art in Prague, its motif being identified from another replica in the Kunstgewerbemuseum in Berlin, is an outstanding creation of his studio.

The development and decline of the dazzling Venetian work is richly represented in Czecho-

16

slovak collections. In Prague, there are also the later variants which, at the beginning of the fourteenth century, found continuity in Sicilian workshops at Palermo.

Only the Umbrian Deruta remained in the first half of the sixteenth century untouched by changing fashions. It profited from the fact that Cesare Borgia, since 1492 the Archbishop of Valencia, was its ruler. Direct contact with the chief centre of the Spanish production of lustered ceramics had enabled Deruta to introduce the long admired technique of the Moorish potters, hitherto kept secret by them, of colours with metallic brilliance. The conception of large dishes of massive biscuit, which are usually covered only on the outer side with tin-glaze, while at the back they have only a leaden transparent one, is for ever connected with the name of the Deruta workshops. The rims are decorated with scale-pattern, severely stylised palmettes, rosettes and tendrils of the early Renaissance style. On the base there are the figures of dreaming girls, reminding one of the languid charm of Perugino's women. Sometimes there are figures of saints, coats of arms or even *genre* scenes, as for instance in the dish from Rožmberk Castle, where in an interior hung with curtains, with a mosaic chequer pavement, a woman in the dress of the period is sitting on a chest. The cool, predominantly blue colouring, the assured drawing, together with a definite iconography, epitomise the specific characteristics of Deruta. The popular Deruta ceramics were made to order, judging by the stock of plaster relief moulds, and this explains why individual kinds frequently occur in series. A dish with the figure of a girl and the inscription NEMO SUA SORTE CHONTENTU 27 from the Museum of Industrial Art in Prague is an exact replica of another piece from a former collection of Charles Antiques; another Prague dish covered with a concentric decor 29 of stylised floral arabesque has its variants in the museums in London and Pesaro. Further, 28 a special cup, adorned with relief moulded scale-pattern and with gold lustre over its whole surface from the Museum of Industrial Art in Prague has its counterpart and a series of variants in the Victoria and Albert Museum in London, where we also find the replica of the Prague relief of Saint Hieronymus with the Lion. 25

Also typical of Deruta ware are decorative two-handled vases with short, narrowed necks, broad rather than high but preserving the stately dignity so typical of all Deruta pieces. An example from the collection of the Museum of Industrial Art in Brno is covered over its 30

entire surface with a fine wall-paper pattern, whereas on the vase from the Červený Kameň
26 Castle the principle motif is a foliage wreath with a heart pierced by a dart.

In Czech collections there are also examples of the early period of Deruta production. These
are two lustreless dishes, painted in deep, brilliant, high-temperature colours. On the rim of the
first, from the Silesian Museum at Opava, palmettes alternate with the scalepattern and on the
base there are the figures of a man and woman in the costumes of that period. The base of
the second, from the collections of the Liberec Museum, is adorned with the figure of a rider.

The workshops in the neighbouring Umbrian Gubbio, too, were famous for their painting
in lustre. They compete with Deruta with their ruby lustre which was invented by the Gubbio
master potter, Giorgio Andreoli. The unusual popularity which this discovery enjoyed throughout Italy induced the local workshops to occupy themselves mainly with finishing other people's products. Perhaps this is the reason why the actual Gubbio style developed eclectically
and that in spite of an unusually extensive production it never attained the unity and
purity of style which characterised the works of neighbouring Deruta. Typical Gubbio
products are the well-known *coppa d'amore*—small, hollow bowls with the figures of girls or
young men whose individually conceived features were captured by the painters most
probably directly from living models. The effective brilliance of the lustre was used by the
Gubbio potters also on small vessels moulded in relief. On a bowl with the figure of Saint
31 Stephen on its concave bottom, from the North Bohemian Museum at Liberec, the decorator
employed contrasting golden and ruby lustre.

Ornament was used independently on majolica ware only very rarely. Usually it created
only the decorative setting of a medieval composition. On vessels from the end of the
fifteenth and the beginning of the sixteenth century the figural theme is more or less only
a coloured drawing and harmonizes with the stylised ornament of the rim. But soon the
workshop decorators started to paint in earnest and in this way brought a completely foreign
element into the sphere of ceramics. Already on a Faenza plate, decorated with the Adora-
11 tion of the Infant Jesus and dated about 1505, from the Museum of Industrial Art in Brno,
the drawing has given way to painting. The colour has lost the freshness of local tone and is
differentiated by lights, achieved through the application of white lead or layers of light

18

opaque colours. In the palette there appear new, until then unknown shades of yellows, greens and the latest addition—violet, obtained by burning manganese.

The painting trend culminates only in the second quarter of the sixteenth century in the decorative *l'art pour l'art* of the Urbino ware. Urbino was the last word in this respect. Patronised by the court, there developed here for more than two decades an original, luxurious production, the subject of which —'historiae'—is the only decoration, suppressing ornament and covering the whole surface of the pieces without regard to their contours. Scenes from ancient   36 mythology—from Ovid's *Metamorphoses* and Livy's *Roman History*—scenes from the Old and the New Testament and the legends of the saints, and less frequently contemporary themes, are the main subjects. As before, painters were inspired by contemporary painting. Whereas at the beginning of the century the Italian Quattrocento artists such as Mantegna, Nicoletto da Modena or Campagnola and Dürer, Beham and Cranach among the Germans, reigned supreme, in the Urbino period the fashion is set by Raphael and his pupils, whose work is spread throughout the ceramic workshops by means of engravings by Marcantonio Raimondi and his circle. Their chief merit consisted in the skilful arrangement of the selected group or an individual figure in a new composition unit and in its successful rendering on the walls of the vessels. Eclectism as a creative method reached its culmination in the works of the Urbino majolica ware painters. Every workshop, every painter mastered a range of selected motifs. This applies equally to so outstanding an artist as the Urbino painter Francesco Xanto Avelli from Rovigo. On the plate with Damocles and Dionysius the Tyrant, from the Museum of   V Industrial Art in Prague, which he signed and dated 1540, are four of the principal motifs which had appeared in his work individually already several years before and again, with variations, later on. The reason why these 'historiae' were so valued in their time does not lie in their originality but in their illustrative interest and iconographic variety and also in the painting itself. The painters perfectly mastered the application of colour on enamel and their execution gave the impression of spontaneity. They knew how to develop the limited scale of high-temperature colours into a rich series of tones, half-tones and shades, and with lead white, by means of which they moulded the shape, they succeeded in achieving an unusual variety of colours and plasticity.

Nicola da Urbino, the Fontana family, Francesco Durantino—these, besides the above-mentioned Xanto Avelli, are among the foremost artists of the famous Urbino period whom we know by their signed works. In the multitude of unsigned Urbino products, painted with equal virtuosity, it is not always easy to deduce their authorship.

The popularity of majolica ware with 'historiae' was unusual in the sixteenth century. Dated, very often signed and bearing short inscriptions on the back, this majolica ware, illustrating in cycles well-known literary subjects, tempted collectors desiring curiosities not only in Italy but also in distant countries. Even in the renowned collection of the Emperor Rudolph II at Prague Castle there were, among other ceramics, about a hundred and eighty majolica pieces of various sizes with 'beautiful historiae'. After Rudolph's death, however, the same destiny befell them as the other Rudolphian collections: for the most part they were lost to Bohemia and transported to Vienna.

41 In the Museum of Industrial Art in Prague, in addition to the plate by Xanto Avelli,
42 already mentioned, there is a large wash-basin with a picture of a boar hunt—a large figural composition after an unknown engraving, applied in a masterly fashion on the bulbous parts
43 of the mantle, a plate featuring Neptune, and another one with a scene of Peleus and Thetis, with a brilliantly carried out painting of muscular men's bodies. Finally there is a pilgrim
VI bottle with pictures from the history of Cain and Abel.

44 Related to them is a beautifully coloured plate showing Judith and Holophernes in the
40 Museum of Industrial Art in Brno with a lively battle scene, and in the North Bohemian Museum at Liberec a bowl with the history of Coriolanus painted by the Xanto Avelli circle of painters. In the same museum there is also a plate with a picture of a landscape and the
46 arms of the Florentine Salviati, perhaps from Fontana's workshop, which is a part of a set represented today by specimens in the Victoria and Albert Museum in London and the
38, 39 Kunstgewerbemuseum in Berlin. A wash-basin with Moses's Miracle of the Water in the Desert from the Červený Kameň Castle.

The Urbino style of painting influenced also other production centres: Pesaro, Faenza, Gubbio and Venice. Faenza 'historiae' are represented in the collections of the Museum of
35 Industrial Art in Prague by a bowl with a scene of Joseph of Egypt meeting his Brothers,

20

signed by Baldasar Manara, the foremost Faenza painter. Venetian origin is recalled here
by a bowl with Diana and Akteon, from the former Lobkowicz Roudnice collection, with   37
characteristic types of women's heads with curly hair, known from contemporary Titian
portraits and appearing also on the albarello with 'Beautiful Cornelia', already mentioned.

In the second half of the century interest in Urbino 'historiae' ceased. Increased imports
of Chinese porcelain turned attention elsewhere, awakening general admiration for the
beauty of plain white or ware slightly decorated with cobalt—an admiration which, in 1575 to
1587, led in Florence to an unsuccessful attempt to manufacture Italian—Medici—porcelain.
The Urbino workshop of the Fontana family and their follower Patanazzi quickly reacted
to the new change of taste. A large bowl with arms on a raised centre from the Prague
Museum of Industrial Art and a similar one with the initials P. A. in the North Bohemian
Museum at Liberec are representative pieces of the Patanazzi workshop style about 1580.   47
On opaque white glazing there appears on them a typical new Urbino decor—small motifs of
phantastic animals and mythological figures, architectural elements and delicate tendrils,
an ornament inspired by the grotesque style of Raphael paintings in the Vatican. On an
albarello from the Silesian Museum at Opava a cartouche with a figural scene is a further
example of this decor.

Due to the manufacture of white majolica Faenza is again coming to the fore. *Bianchi di
Faenza*—faience, as it is called in France after the town it made famous—is produced there in   55
the form of large numbers of dinner services, trays, sauce-boats, salt cellars, candlesticks,
bottles, and so on. Its biscuit is relatively thin, its shapes are often well formed in plaster
moulds, and its thick layer of glazing has an opaque white tone. The decor painted in light
cobalt, yellow and brown manganese, consists of a thin formal tendril and of figures of putti,   54
saints or other figural motifs, and it is lightly sketched in the flowing style which has given its   50
name to a whole group of majolica thus decorated. The succinct sketchy style—*stil compendiario*—   51
is connected with the production of the workshops of Vigilioto Calamelli, his successor Giovanni
Bettisi called Don Pino and Domenicus Pirotti, whose works are extensively represented both   48, 49
by signed and unsigned works in the collections of the Museum of Industrial Art in Prague
and Brno as well as in the Červený Kameň Castle.   52

The change which took place at this time in the production of majolica was not only a short-lived fashion. The use of white, easily washable vessels for everyday use, instead of metal ones or technically less perfect kinds of earthenware, was a mark of progress in the hygiene of tableware which thus set the path leading up to the present day. We can, therefore, consider white majolica as one of the lasting contributions of the period to the development of European civilization. In the second half of the sixteenth century majolica ware was employed for such domestic use not only in Italy and the whole of Central Europe but also in the lands of Bohemia where humanistic education, manners, taste and the fashion of Italian Renaissance culture had prepared the ground well for a new expansion of local social culture. Italian majolica appeared there as one of the signs of the new artistic orientation of the Czech nobility as well as of the city patricians who found in foreign ware and artistic creations of all kinds a medium not only of personal representation but also a gratification of their growing aesthetic need and love of luxury. Two large, unfortunately incomplete majolica dinner services from the Lobkowicz Castle at Roudnice, now partially deposited in the Museum of Industrial Art in Prague and in the Museum at Mělník, are a rare period relic. They were made either directly at Faenza or by Italian potters who emigrated to Bohemia. The former service, dating from the eighties of the sixteenth century, bears the arms of Vratislav of Pernštejn, the High Chancellor of the Kingdom of Bohemia, and his wife Maximiliana Manrique de Lara de Mendoza; the latter, from a later era, is decorated with the arms of the Megava House. Unfortunately nothing has been preserved from the collections of white as well as decorated Italian majolica ware which are mentioned in the inventories of rich Prague patricians from the last decade of the sixteenth century and which disappeared, together with all the riches accumulated in the towns, during the war years of the next century.

White Italian majolica ware is very important in the cultural history of many countries because the local faience work was inspired by it. France, Switzerland, Germany and the Netherlands, as well as Bohemia learned from Italian potters the art of using tin glaze and soon these countries were self-supporting in the production of faience. They became a dangerous competitor to the Italians who, about 1600, slowly lost their leading position. Italy began, in fact, to benefit from other countries' artistic and technical contributions to the art.

But the colourful Urbino style was maintained in an even cheaper form in second-rate workshops long into the seventeenth century. The same also applied to Urbino grotesques, which still at the end of the eighteenth century appeared for example on a group of Pesara jugs from the workshop of Ant. Casali and Fil. Ant. Callegari, though the workmanship did not equal that of the past. These later samples as well as majolica pieces with plant ornaments and trophies in 'archaic' style, dating from the turn of the sixteenth and seventeenth centuries, are widely represented in the Czech collections. In the Museum of Industrial Art in Prague there is a group of drug-pots from Palermo from the beginning of the seventeenth century with formal plant decor arranged in stripes, with cartouches and heads of Turks and a characteristically dull colouring.

From all the majolica production in the seventeenth century only that of a few little-known workshops is outstanding. From 1620—1660 the Toscana Montelupo is the name to remember. In the Museum of Industrial Art in Prague and in the Červený Kameň Castle their majolica VII is represented by a series of dishes of an unusually effective, lively colouring, with period figures wittily caricatured, which testify to the extraordinary artistic originality of their creators.

The blue-white style of Chinese porcelain was being imported to Europe in increasing quantity. This is represented in Italy by especially characteristic Ligurian majolica in the 53 second half of the seventeenth century. In the Prague Museum of Industrial Art the whole 56 development of these ceramics is represented by the creations of the Pescetto, Chiodo and Giordano workshops at Savona. There are dishes there with mythological scenes, painted with cobalt in bold brush-work, as well as works from the end of the century, such as plates, dishes, 59 trays, tea pots and *terrines*, frequently moulded in relief or pierced in openwork, with white, lustrous glazing, decorated with sketches of landscapes, plant, animal and Cupid motifs. 57 These include in Telč Castle a beautiful, signed, ribbed Savona bottle with a tin stopper, small deer and birds in blue and a similarly decorated, also signed, Savona jug of melon shape from the Museum of Industrial Art in Prague.

About 1700, ceramic workshops at Bassano and Angarano in the Venetian region come to the fore. The production of these ateliers is represented by several sets of pieces from the original Lobkowicz estate at Roudnice, today deposited in the Museum of Industrial Art in Prague and in the Mělník Museum. The silvery, lustrous, grey glaze of its vessels, the stereotype, 'antique' style landscapes, painted in dull tones of blue, green and yellow and brown manganese, brought to Italian production a characteristic note. This is especially true of the dishes, decorated on the rim by an acanthus trailing decor moulded in relief, such as on the Prague Neptune dish, and shows to what extent the Venetian majolica paid tribute to period taste and contemporary works wrought of silver.

Castelli of Abruzzi was the last workshop which extended the artistic tradition of Italian majolica far into the eighteenth century. It first drew attention to itself at the beginning of the seventeenth century with a small group of blue-painted majolica ware, represented in the North Bohemian Museum at Liberec by a plate with a picture of Judith with the head of Holophernes. It is interesting historically because the arms of the Bohemian House of Wallenstein are depicted on the formal plant rim. It is a part of a set, two further pieces of which, each with a different motif, are in the Victoria and Albert Museum in London. Another specimen of this group, without arms, but also with Judith's picture, and related by the whole character of its painting to the Prague plate, is in the Museum für Kunst und Gewerbe in Hamburg.

The style of the Castello workshops crystallized after the first half of the seventeenth century in a colourful painting of figural compositions, compiled from early baroque graphic art. A dish with a rider on a rearing horse from the Červený Kameň Castle, a dish with a falconer and the sign of Gemini from the Museum at Liberec, a plate with a beautifully painted scene of two embracing nude women from the Rožmberk Castle and two others with the sign of Pisces and Sagittarius from the Prague Museum of Industrial Art are outstanding examples of this group, the common characteristic of which, besides the discreet colouring, is the typical acanthus trailing decor on the rims of the dishes.

The tradition of Italian figural painting culminates in Castelli in the first half of the eighteenth century in the members of the families of the painters Grue and Gentile. Landscape genres in the style of Bergham and Bassano and religious scenes, inspired by contemporary Italian baroque graphic art, a harmonious colouring of pale tones, contrasted to the dark

24

brown of manganese and masterly luminous painting—these are the characteristic signs of this late style which in the collections of the Prague Museum of Industrial Art is represented by black specimens, particularly two large albarellos with praying monks, one of these pieces 68 being signed by Dr Fr. X. Grue.

This period of the Castello workshops ends the history of the artistic development of Italian majolica. In the course of the eighteenth century there arose, it is true, in northern Italy a number of ceramic workshops—in Milan, Turin, Treviso, Modena and Nove. All of them, 64 however, gradually abandoned the traditions of Italian majolica ware and began to compete with a new ceramic material—porcelain—which they imitated not only in the decor but also in the painting technique of enamel colours on glaze.

Every pioneering and creative work, being an expression of its period and the individuality of its creator, can be imitated up to a point—but an echo will never recall to life the first inner urgency and persuasiveness. Thus the best attempts of the Ginori and Cantabello workshops in the second half of the nineteenth century, were unsuccessful. The renaissance of Italian majolica ware, though a commercial success, was not an artistic triumph.

LIST OF PLATES

1. Vessel with handles. Pastose cobalt blue painting of oak foliage and lily blossom on greyish white glaze. Height 20 cm. Florence, second quarter of the 15th century.

   Liberec, North Bohemian Museum

2. Deep bowl with the arms of probably the Baglioni family of Perugia in a wreath of stylised foliage on the bottom. Painted in inky blackish-blue, orange and copper green. On the under side of rim blue loops with stars, with orange dots between rays. Diam. 265 cm. Faenza, 1490—1500.

   Opava, Silesian Museum (Inv. No. 03.232)

3. Vessel with bust of man in antique helmet in a foliage wreath. White glaze with high lustre. Painted in deep blackish-blue, orange, yellow and copper green. H. 29.5 cm. Faenza, 1480—1500. *Prague, Museum of Industrial Art (Inv. No. 279)*

4. Plate with the motif of a running hare in a rectangular panel on the bottom. Painted in inky blackish-blue, yellow, orange and copper green. Diam. 26.5 cm. Florence (?), about 1500. *Opava, Silesian Museum (Inv. No. 40 332)*

5. Drug-pot, albarello, with the inscription B. MARCIATO and a design of leaf tendrils with blossoms. Painted in deep blue and brownish orange. H. 18.5 cm.

   Prague, Museum of Industrial Art (Inv. No. 4439)

6. Pharmaceutical jug with the inscription DIAMORON in a foliage wreath with fruit, with acanthus leaves design and rosettes in reserve on coloured background. Yellowish white glaze, blue drawing, painted in green, yellow orange, yellow and blue. Glued. H. 25 cm. Deruta (?), 1510—1520.

   Prague, Museum of Industrial Art (Inv. No. 1107)

7. Relief with The Adoration of the Three Kings with figures in dress of the period. On the load of a lying camel there is a shield of arms displaying an eagle with crown. Painted in two shades in green, orange, yellow, blue and brown manganese. Dimensions 73×66.5 cm. Faenza, about 1525.

   Prague, Museum of Industrial Art (Inv. No. D 1191/6)

8. Drug-pot with the inscription A. DE EUFRAGIE, with a picture of Kimon and Pera. White glaze with high lustre. Painted in rich blue, lemon yellow, copper green and white. H. 44 cm. Faenza or Caffaggiolo, 1525–1530.

Prague, Museum of Industrial Art (Inv. No. 277)

9. Drug-pot with the inscription A. DE BUGLOSSA, with a picture of Lucretia and the heraldic lily of Florence. Colouring the same as in the preceding item. H. 44 cm. Faenza or Caffaggiolo, 1525–1530. *Prague, Museum of Industrial Art (Inv. No. 278)*

10. Plate with an emblem in which, under a crown, a man's and a woman's hands are clasped above a flame. Calligraphic decor on the back. The decor in reserve on a rich blue background. Signed ⟨mark⟩ Diam. 25.5 cm. Faenza, about 1525.

Brno, Museum of Industrial Art (Inv. No. 9490)

11. Plate with The Adoration of the Christ Child on the bottom, with fruit draperies, dolphins and winged dragons on the rim. The centre painted in yellow, olive green, violet manganese and white. Decor of the rim in reserve on a dark blue background. On the back, orange scale-pattern with blue spirals and frieze with a blue tendril. On the bottom a rosette. Diam. 24.5 cm. Faenza, about 1505.

Brno, Museum of Industrial Art (Inv. No. 9488)

12. Plate with light blue glaze and bust of man in helmet and the inscription ALESĀDR on the bottom. The rim decorated with 'a berettino' grotesques. The centre painted yellow, orange and white. On the under side close-set concentric blue circles. Diam. 24.5 cm. Faenza, Casa Pirota, 1535–1540.

Brno, Museum of Industrial Art (Inv. No. 9494)

13. Wash-basin with light blue glaze decorated on the surface with 'a berettino' grotesques and trophies. In front and on the back the arms of the Florentine Salviati family, painted in yellow, orange and green. On the bottom of the basin a decor of fruit and leaves, similarly painted. Diam. 35 cm, height 15 cm. The basin is part of a Salviati set, some items of which, dated 1531, are in the Victoria and Albert Museum in London and in the R. Qualino Collection in Turin. Faenza, Casa Pirota, 1531. *Brno, Museum of Industrial Art, (Inv. No. 9489)*

14. Pilgrim-bottle, star-shaped, with grey blue glaze, with stylised plant motifs, painted in yellow, orange, copper green, dark blue and white. H. 27.5 cm. Faenza or Venice, about 1550. *Prague, Museum of Industrial Art (Inv. No. 11.558)*

15. Plate covered with a light blue glaze, decorated with *a berettino* grotesques, and the figure of a lute-player in the middle, painted in orange, yellow-green and white. On the back close-set concentric blue bands. Diam. 24.5 cm. Faenza, Casa Pirota, dated 1540. *Prague, Museum of Industrial Art (Inv. No. 3897)*

16. Dish covered with dark blue glaze, bottom moulded in relief, with a shield of arms on the raised bottom. Painted in yellow, green, orange-brown, white and blackish-blue. On the back, yellow tendril with black-blue trefoils. Diam. 42 cm. Venice (?), 1530—1540. *Brno, Museum of Industrial Art (Inv. No. 9491)*

17. Dish with rim moulded in relief in oblique grooves, alternately rich blue and orange, with acanthus leaves in reserve. On the bottom the figure of an Apostle in a landscape, painted in blue, orange, copper green and white. On the back, grooves separated by blue bands alternately decorated with yellow and brown leaf tendrils. Diam. 29 cm. Faenza, about 1535.
Liberec, North Bohemian Museum (Inv. No. J I 15)

18. Dish with Archangel Michael fighting the devil, painted in yellow, orange, blue, green, violet and black-brown manganese. On the rim ornament in *bianco sopra bianco*. Glued. Diam. 46.5 cm. Castel Durante, 1535—1540.
Brno, Museum of Industrial Art (Inv. No. 9492)

19. Vessel with *a trofei* decor, painted *en grisaille* in yellow-green and grey-green on a brilliant blue background. H. 29 cm. Castel Durante, dated 1565.
Liberec, North Bohemian Museum (Inv. No. F 1)

20. Drug-pot, albarello, with the inscription SYO EPITIME and a Turk's head. Ornament in blue contours in reserve on a background alternately painted in rich blue, brownish orange and copper green. H. 32 cm. Faenza (?), about 1550.
Prague, Museum of Industrial Art (Inv. No. 281)

28

21. Albarello with three reserves in floral decor, in reserves are bust of woman with the inscription CORNELIA BELLA, head of a white-bearded man and bust of woman and beneath her the inscription MOSTARD in cartouche. Painted in deep blue, copper green, yellow, orange, violet manganese and white. H. 42 cm. Venice, the workshop of Domenico da Venezia, about 1560—1580.

Prague, Museum of Industrial Art (Inv. No. 2087)

22. Bowl. The bottom with facets in relief the surfaces of which are alternately dark blue, orange, green and in yellowish-white glaze. On the back, yellow and blue bands. Diam. 25 cm. Faenza, about 1535.

Opava, Silesian Museum (Inv. No. 03.231)

23. Deep plate covered with grey-blue glaze, with dark blue maple leaves and, on the bottom, the arms of the Florentine Minerbetti family, painted in orange-brown. On the back, thin blue interlaced motives round the centre. Diam. 21.3 cm. Venice, 1540—1550. *Červený Kameň State Castle (Inv. No. ČK 2522)*

24. Bowl covered with grey-blue glaze and maple leaves painted in dark blue and white. On the back, a wreath of pointed foliage. Diam. 29 cm. Venice, 1540—1550.

Prague, Museum of Industrial Art (Inv. No. 7603)

25. Relief of St Jerome with lion. Painted in blue, yellow-orange and gold lustre. Dimensions 26×21 cm. Gubbio or Deruta, 1510—1520.

Prague, Museum of Industrial Art (Inv. No. 2110)

26. Vase, with two handles, with the emblem of a heart pierced with an arrow. Drawing in blue, painted in brassy yellow lustre. Foot restored. H. 26.5 cm. Deruta, about 1530. *Červený Kameň State Castle (Inv. No. ČK 2499)*

27. Dish with a bust of girl and inscription NEMO SUA SORTE CHONTENTU. Painted in blue and brassy yellow lustre. On the back transparent yellowish lead glaze. Diam. 40 cm. Deruta, about 1520.

Prague, Museum of Industrial Art (Inv. No. 5205)

28. Cup with scales applied in relief, decorated with brassy yellow lustre. H. 21 cm. Deruta, about 1520. *Prague, Museum of Industrial Art (Inv. No. 11.559)*

29. Dish with stylised floral decor composed round the centre with a pelican in a round medallion on the bottom. Yellowish glaze. Painted in blue and brassy yellow lustre. On the back uncoloured lead glaze. Diam. 41.5 cm. Deruta, about 1530.

Prague, Museum of Industrial Art (Inv. No. 2633)

30. Vase with two handles and similar decor. Painted in blue and brassy yellow lustre. The foot glued. H. 25 cm. Deruta, about 1530.

Brno, Museum of Industrial Art (Inv. No. 24.700)

31. Bowl with the picture of St Sebastian. Painted in blue, rim decorated with brassy yellow and ruby lustre. On the back, yellowish lustre with disc motive. Diam. 29 cm. Gubbio, 1530–1535. *Liberec, North Bohemian Museum (Inv. No. J I 14)*

32. Plate with stylised floral decor on the bottom and on the radially divided rim. Rose-coloured glaze. Painted in blue with yellow and ruby lustre. On the back, seven carmine and yellow bands. Diam. 23.5 cm. Gubbio, 1520–1530.

Prague, Museum of Industrial Art (Inv. No. 11.560)

33. Dish with figures of man and woman in costumes of the period. Painted in deep blue, orange, yellow, copper green and grey green. On the back uncoloured lead glaze. Diam. 40 cm. Deruta, 1540–1550.

Opava, Silesian Museum (Inv. No. U O 1254)

34. Bowl from an accouchement set. In an interior scene women are playing with a child. Painted in blue, three shades of green, yellow, orange, violet and black-brown manganese and white. On the lid of the bowl a scene illustrating the serving of food to the mother who is lying in bed. On the back a running putto holding the globe. Diam. 22 cm. Castel Durante, 1525–1530.

Prague, Museum of Industrial Art (Inv. No. 285)

35. Bowl, on foot, with the figure of Joseph of Egypt finding a gold cup in Benjamin's bag. Painted in vivid blue, copper and yellow-green, yellow, orange and white. On the back orange scale pattern, on the bottom the signature: BALDASSARE MANARA. Diam. 23.5 cm. Faenza, painted by Baldassare Manara, about 1535.

Prague, Museum of Industrial Art (Inv. No. 273)

36. Bowl with an illustration of the rape of Ganymede by the eagle. Painted in blue, green, several shades of orange, violet and brown-black manganese and white. On the back the inscription: GANIMEDE. Diam. 27 cm. Urbino, 1535—1540.

37. Bowl with the Judgment of Paris. Painted in blue, green, yellow and violet manganese. On the back a blue wreath, tendrils with leaves and on the bottom the inscription: LALTO GIUDITIO DEL TROIAN PASTORE. S. 61. Diam. 29,5 cm. Urbino, 1540—1550. *Opava, Silesian Museum (Inv. No. 10/98)*

38.—39. Wash-basin with Moses' miracle of the water in the desert. On the outside sea-side landscape with sailing-vessels and cupola architecture. Painted in blue, several shades of green, yellow, orange, violet manganese and white. On the back of the bottom, the inscription: E QUANDO MOSE PER VIRTU DI DIO FECE SORTIRE L'AQUA DALLA PIETRA. ENN. Diam. 39 cm, height 17 cm. Urbino, 1540—1550. *Červený Kameň State Castle (Inv. No. ČK 2480)*

40. Bowl, on foot, with a scene from the story of Coriolanus. Painted in blue, two shades of green, typical scale of yellows, in violet and brown-black manganese and white. On the back three yellow bands. On the bottom the inscription: CORIOLANO ROMANO. Diam. 26 cm. Urbino, attributed to the workshop of Francesco Xanto Avelli da Rovigo, about 1540.

Liberec, North Bohemian Museum (Inv. No. J I 48)

41. Wash-basin with boar hunt. On the outside surface rocky sea-side landscape, on the back of the bottom a dolphin in waves. Painted in three shades of green, yellow, brown-orange, blue and violet and brown-black manganese and white. Glued. Diam. 37.5 cm. H. 12.5 cm. Urbino, 1540—1540.

Prague, Museum of Industrial Art (Inv. No. 8875)

42. Plate with Neptune on a shell drawn on the sea by dolphins. Painted in the usual scale of high temperature colours, violet manganese is missing. On the back of the rim three yellow bands. On the bottom the inscription: NETTUNO IN CASTRO/NE, 1544. Diam. 24.5 cm. Urbino, probably Francesco Durantino, 1544.

43. Bowl with scenes from the story of Peleus and Thetis. Painted in the usual scale o high-temperature colours, yellow and orange prevailing, and in grey-brown manganese. On the back of rim two orange bands, on the bottom the inscription: PELEO A TETIS IN VARIE FO/RME 1546. Diam. 26.5 cm. Urbino, attributed to the Fontana workshop, 1546.

Prague, Museum of Industrial Art, (Inv. No. 11.573)

44. Bowl on low foot. Judith killing Holophernes and a skirmish. Painted in high-temperature colours, with a special application of red-orange and violet and brown-black manganese. On the bottom of the vessel the inscription: ODITA AMACO LO/FERNES FATO IN PE/SARO 1544. Diam. 28 cm. Pesaro, 1544.

Brno, Museum of Industrial Art (Inv. No. 8778)

45. Plate, grey blue glaze, with sea-side landscape, buildings and ships. Painted in dark blue, green and yellow. On the back a blue tendril with leaves. On the bottom the inscription: 1548 ADI 18-MAIO.FAVO. Diam. 28.5 cm. Venice, 1548.

Opava, Silesian Museum (Inv. No. 03.230)

46. Deep plate with two wading men in a landscape and the arms of the Florentine Salviati family. Painted in blue, several shades of green, yellow, orange and brown-black manganese. On the back three yellow bands. Diam. 24 cm. Urbino, attributed to the Orazio Fontana workshop, about 1560.

Liberec, North Bohemian Museum (Inv. No. J I 13)

47. Dish with grotesques and an unascertained coat of arms on a raised bottom. Yellow-white glaze. Painted in grey blue, yellow, orange and brown manganese. Diam. 46 cm. Urbino, in the Patanazzi style, 1580—1600.

Prague, Museum of Industrial Art (Inv. No. 7065)

48. Bowl, openwork, with a sketchy drawing of a walking putto in the middle. Painted in grey-blue, orange and yellow. Diam. 23 cm. Faenza, probably the workshop of Domenico Pirotti, last quarter of the 16th century.

Prague, Museum of Industrial Art (Inv. No. Z 100/84)

49. Oval dish moulded in relief with the figure of Poseidon riding on a dolphin and the mono-

gram G TO. Painted in grey blue, orange and violet-brown manganese. Dimensions 35×30.4 cm. Faenza, signed Don Pino, last quarter of the 16th century.

Červený Kameň State Castle (Inv. No. ČK 2533)

50. Pilgrim-bottle, moulded in relief with an unascertained coat of arms and the monogram C. V. K. between crossed sprigs. Painted in grey-blue, yellow and brown manganese. H. 37 cm. Faenza, about 1600.

Prague, Museum of Industrial Art (Inv. No. 11.566)

51. Jug, ribbed, with the arms of Ferdinand II and Anna Eleonora Gonzaga. Painted in brown manganese, in orange and grey-blue. Height 28 cm. Faenza or Urbino, after the year 1622. *Prague, Museum of Industrial Art (Inv. No. 11.567)*

52. Wash-basin with the arms of Piccolomini and the device VIX SEPARABIT MORS. Painted in grey-blue, orange-brown, yellow. On the bottom a wreath of blue lobed foliage. Signed ᴅᴏᴘɪ Diam. 31.5 cm, h. 13 cm. Faenza, Don Pino workshop, about 1580. *Opava, Silesian Museum (Inv. No. 27, 13)*

53. Bowl moulded in relief with a horse in the middle. Painted in grey-blue, yellow, grey-green and violet manganese. Glued. Diam. 43 cm. Montelupo. 1630—1660.

Prague, Museum of Industrial Art (Inv. No. 28.054)

54. Jardinière with handles in the shape of winged Naiads with shells and painted putti. Painted in the same colours as the previous item with added olive green. Glued. H. 16 cm. Urbino or Faenza, 1580—1600.

Prague, Museum of Industrial Art (Inv. No. Z 98/19)

55. Sauce-boat moulded in the form of a mermaid, holding a shell. White glaze. Height 12.5 cm. Faenza or Urbino, third quarter of the 16th century.

Prague, Museum of Industrial Art (Inv. No. 11.583)

56. Bottle in the shape of double busts of man and woman in costumes of the period. Crackled greyish glaze. Painted in yellow, grey-blue, olive green and brown-violet manganese. H. 26.5 cm. Montelupo, about 1660.

Prague, Museum of Industrial Art (Inv. No. Z 215)

57. Bowl, openwork, with a sketch of a flying putto and landscapes, painted in cobalt blue.

On the back signed ![signature mark] Diam. 29.6 cm. Savona, Levantino workshop,
about 1670.   *Prague, Museum of Industrial Art (Inv. No. Z 209/20)*

58. Dish with silver-grey glaze, moulded in relief, with the figure of Neptune in a carriage
drawn by sea-horses. Painted in blue, orange, grey-green and brown-violet
manganese. Dimensions 48×39 cm. Bassano, 1680—1700.
   Prague, Museum of Industrial Art (Inv. No. Z 209/25)

59. Bowl with bluish-white glaze with a sketch of Cupid and woman pursued by man,
painted in cobalt blue. On the back, blue sketches. On the bottom signed
Diam. 30 cm. Savona, Levantino workshop, about 1670.
   Prague, Museum of Industrial Art (Inv. No. D 1328/39)

60. Plate with Judith holding the head of Holophernes and the arms of the Wallenstein
family, painted in cobalt blue. Diam. 23.5 cm. Castelli, 1610—1620.
   Liberec, North Bohemian Museum (Inv. No. J I 25)

61. Dish with a view of a Baroque garden and a falconer. Painted in grey blue, yellow orange,
yellow green and brownish violet manganese. Diam. 34.5 cm. Castelli 1680—1700.
   Liberec, North Bohemian Museum (Inv. No. J I 47)

62. Small plate with sunset in a romantic landscape. Painted in the same colour scheme as
the preceding item, yellow green shades prevailing. Diam. 18 cm. Castelli, about
1740.   *Prague, Museum of Industrial Art (Inv. No. 2809)*

63. Drug-pot, albarello, with the figure of a praying monk and the inscription: PER SM.
CRUCEM LIBERATI SUMUS. H. 27 cm, diam. 21.5 cm. Castelli, signed
Dr F. A. X. Grue, about 1735.
   Prague, Museum of Industrial Art (Inv. No. 1110)

64. Plate with Rococo decor in the chinoiserie style. Painted in grey-blue, olive green, orange
and brownish violet manganese. Diam. 23.5 cm. Nove, Pasqual Antonibon period,
about 1750.   *Prague, Museum of Industrial Art (Inv. No. 1880)*

COLOUR PLATES

I. Jug with bird. On the surface greyish white glaze; inside and on the foot transparent yellow lead glaze. Manganese drawing; painted in copper green. Height 36 cm. Orvieto or Faenza, beginning of the 15th century.

Opava, Silesian Museum (Inv. No. ST 4)

II. Vessel with a bird in a wreath, on the back an asymmetrical decor of large leaves. Greyish white glaze. Painted in slate, blackish-blue, orange and brownish orange with copper green and violet manganese. H. 33 cm. Florence or Faenza. 1450—1470.

Brno, Museum of Industrial Art (Inv. No. 1514)

III. Dish with a rider in Roman armour, scale-pattern and palmette decor on the rim. Painted in rich blue, yellow-orange, sulphur yellow and copper green. On the back yellowish transparent lead glaze. Diam. 37 cm. Deruta, about 1525.

Liberec, North Bohemian Museum (Inv. No. F 13)

IV. Bottom of a bowl covered with light blue glaze, with the picture of Christ and a Samaritan woman. Painted in yellow, orange, green, red-brown to ochre and white. On the back, dark blue wavy stems and rosettes. Glued. Diam. 22 cm. Faenza, Casa Pirota, about 1525.

Prague, Museum of Industrial Art (Inv. No. Z 263/371)

V. Bowl with the subject of Damocles and the tyrant Dionysius. Painted in blue, yellow, orange, orange-brown, yellow and copper green, violet and brown-black manganese and white. On the back four yellow bands. Signed   Diam. 30 cm. Urbino, painted by Francesco Xanto Avelli da Rovigo,   dated 1540.

Prague, Museum of Industrial Art (Inv. No. 11.571)

VI. Pilgrim-bottle with the subject of Cain killing Abel. On the other side the sacrifices of Cain and Abel. Painted in blue, yellow-green, yellow-orange, red-brown, brown-black and white. H. 40 cm. Urbino, 1540—1550.

Prague, Museum of Industrial Art (Inv. No. Z 97/61)

VII. Dish with the figure of man in broad-brimmed hat with sabres. Painted in rich yellow, blue, orange, copper green and black-brown manganese. On the back three violet bands. Diam. 43.2 cm. Montelupo, about 1630.

Prague, Museum of Industrial Art (Inv. No. Z 242/25)

VIII. Small plate with the scene of Annunciation. Painted in yellow green, light brown-orange, light yellow, olive green, light grey-blue and dark brown manganese. Diam. 17 cm. Castelli, 1750—1760.

Liberec, North Bohemian Museum (Inv. No. J I 26)

BIBLIOGRAPHY

Fr. Morávek, *Nově objevený inventář rudolfinských sbírek. Památky Archeologické, 1923*

Karel Teige, *Základy místopisu pražského*, Prague

Zimmermann, *Das Inventar der Prager Schatz und Kunstkammer vom 1621. Jahrbuch der Kunsthistorischer Sammlungen der allerhöchster Kaiserhauses. XIII—LXXV*

F. Argnani, *Le ceramiche e maioliche faentine.* Faenza *1889*

G. Ballardini, *Corpus della maiolica italiana. I.—II.* Rome *1938*

G. Ballardini, *La maiolica italiana della origine alla fine del cinquencento.* Florence *1938*

W. Bode, *Die Anfänge Majolikakunst in Toskana.* Berlin *1911*

E. W. Braun, *Steirische Wappenschüssern des 16.—17. Jahrhundert. Freunde der Schweizer Keramik, 1950*

L. de Mauri, *L'Amatore di maioliche e porcellane.* Milan *1914*

M. Dvořák a Boh. Matějka, *Soupis památek historických a politických v politickém okresu Roudnickém.* Prague *1907*

Faenza, *Bollettino del Museo delle céramiche in Faenza*

O. Falke, *Majolika.* Berlin *1896*

O. Falke, *Katalog der italienischen Majoliken. Sammlung Richard Zachille.* Leipzig *1899*

O. Falke, *Die Majolikasammlung Alfred Pringsheim, I.—II.* Berlin-Leiden, *1914*

W. B. Honey, *European Ceramic Art. Illustrated historical survey.* London, *1949*

W. B. Honey, *European Ceramic Art. A Dictionary of factories, artists, technical terms etc.* London *1952*

W. B. Honey, *Later italian maiolica. Apollo, VIII (1928)*

Illustrierte Geschichte des Kunstgewerbes. Berlin *1907*

J. Leisching, *Das Erzherzog Rainer Museum für Kunst und Gewerbe in Brünn*, Vienna *1913*

J. Leisching, *Sammlung Lanna Prag I.* Leipzig *1909*

A. Minghetti, *Enciclopedia Biograpfica. XLI. Ceramisti.* Milan *1939*

A. R. Perez, *Maiolica siciliena. L'Arte, XLII (1939)*

G. D. Picolpasso, *I tre libri del'arte del vasajo.* Pesaro *1879*

B. Rackham, *Catalogue of Italian Maiolica, I.—II.* London *1940*

B. Rackham, *Bemerkungen über eine Gruppe italienischer Majoliken des 17. Jahrhunderts. Der Cicerone, XVIII (1926)*

A. del Vite, *Le ceramiche a riflessi della collezione Mazza e la questione delle attribuzioni a Pesaro e Deruta. Le Arti, XIX (1940—1941)*

J. Vydrová, *Italská majolika, v Uměleckoprůmyslovém museu v Praze.* Prague, *1955*

B. Zboińska-Daszyńska, *Majoliki Włoskie.* Cracow *1952*

PLATES

II. FLORENCE OR FAENZA. 1450—1470

9. FAENZA OR CAFFAGGIOLO. 1525—1530

10. FAENZA, ABOUT 1525

11. FAENZA. ABOUT 1505

12. FAENZA, CASA PIROTA. 1535—1540

13. FAENZA, CASA PIROTA. 1531

14. FAENZA OR VENICE. 1550

III. DERUTA. ABOUT 1525

15. FAENZA, CASA PIROTA, 1540

16. VENICE (?). 1530—1540

17. FAENZA. ABOUT 1535

18. CASTEL DURANTE. 1535—1540

19. CASTEL DURANTE. 1565

20. FAENZA (?). ABOUT 1550

21. VENICE, WORKSHOP OF DOMENICO DA VENEZIA. 1560—1580

22. FAENZA. ABOUT 1535

23. VENICE. 1540—1550

24. VENICE. 1540—1550

IV. FAENZA, CASA PIROTA. ABOUT 1525

25. GUBBIO OR DERUTA. 1510—1520

26. DERUTA. ABOUT 1530

27. DERUTA. ABOUT 1520

28. DERUTA. ABOUT 1520

V. URBINO, FRANCESCO XANTO AVELLI OF ROVIGO. 1540

29, DERUTA, ABOUT 1530

30. DERUTA. ABOUT 1530

31. GUBBIO. 1530—1535

32. GUBBIO. 1520—1530

33. DERUTA. 1540—1550

34. CASTEL DURANTE. 1525—1530

35. FAENZA, BALDASSARE MANARA. ABOUT 1535

36. URBINO. 1535—1540

VI. URBINO. 1540—1550

37. URBINO. 1540—1550

38. URBINO. 1540—1550

39. URBINO. 1540—1550

40. URBINO, FRANCESCO XANTO AVELLI DA ROVIGO (?). ABOUT 1540

41. URBINO. 1530—1540

42. URBINO, FRANCESCO DURANTINO (?). 1544

VII. MONTELUPO. SECOND QUARTER OF THE SEVENTEENTH CENTURY

43. URBINO, WORKSHOP OF FONTANO (?). 1546

44. PESARO. 1544

45. VENICE. 1548

46. URBINO, WORKSHOP OF ORAZIO FONTANA (?), ABOUT 1560

47. URBINO, WORKSHOP OF PATANAZZI 1580—1600

48. FAENZA, WORKSHOP OF DOMENICO PIROTTI. END OF THE SIXTEENTH CENTURY

VIII. CASTELLI. 1750—1760

49. FAENZA, WORKSHOP OF DON PINO. LAST QUARTER OF THE SIXTEENTH CENTURY

50. FAENZA. ABOUT 1600

51. FAENZA OR URBINO. AFTER 1622

VIX·SEPARABIT·MORS

52. FAENZA, WORKSHOP OF DON PINO, ABOUT 1580

53. MONTELUPO. 1630—1660

54. URBINO OR FAENZA. 1580—1600

55. FAENZA OR URBINO. THIRD QUARTER OF THE SIXTEENTH CENTURY

56. MONTELUPO. ABOUT 1660

57. SAVONA, WORKSHOP OF LEVANTINO. ABOUT 1670

58. BASSANO. 1680—1700

59. SAVONA, WORKSHOP OF LEVANTINO. ABOUT 1670

60. CASTELLI. 1610—1620

61. CASTELLI. 1680—1700

62. CASTELLI. ABOUT 1740

PER S.ᴹ CRꞶ
CEM LIBE-
RATI SꞶ
MꞶS.
Dꞟ J·A·X·Grꞟꞟ

63. CASTELLI. DR F. A. X. GRUE. ABOUT 1735

64. NOVE. PASQUAL ANTONIBON PERIOD. ABOUT 1750

Printed in Czechoslovak